Crash, Bang, Boom!

Written by Sarah Snashall

Illustrated by Jeff Crowther

Bella, Alexa and Ashok sing a song with Miss Hicks.

The song is sweet.
The children sing it well.

Jack thinks the song is dull.
He gets a drum.

Miss Hicks sighs.
The drum is not a good plan.

Janaki sees Jack with the drum.
She gets a bell.

Max gets a kazoo.

Miss Hicks grits her teeth.

Miss Hicks groans.

Miss Hicks grins.

Wait! Jack still has the drum.

Talk about the story

Ask your child these questions:

1 What were the children doing at the beginning of the story?

2 Who was banging the drum?

3 What other noisy instruments did the children play?

4 How did Miss Hicks feel?

5 What instruments do you enjoy playing?

6 What songs do you enjoy singing?

Can your child retell the story using their own words?